An A-Maze-ing Colorful Mystery

Whodunit
MAZES

Roger Moreau

Sterling Publishing Co., Inc.
New York

This book is dedicated to Eric, Donna, Karen, Sandy

1   3   5   7   9   10   8   6   4   2

Published by Sterling Publishing Company, Inc.

387 Park Avenue South, New York, NY 10016

© 2005 by Roger Moreau

Distributed in Canada by Sterling Publishing

C/o Canadian Manda Group, 165 Dufferin Street

Toronto, Ontario, Canada M6K 3H6

Distributed in Great Britain and Europe by Chris Lloyd at Orca Book Services,

Stanley House, Fleets Lane, Poole BH15 3AJ, England

Distributed in Australia by Capricorn Link (Australia) Pty. Ltd.

P.O. Box 704, Windsor, NSW 2756 Australia

Printed in China

Sterling ISBN 1-4027-1551-X

Contents

Suggested Use of This Book

As you work your way through the pages of this book, try not to mark them up. This will enable you to work at solving this crime over and over again, and will also give your friends a chance to see if they have the same skills and insights you have.

Special Warning: When the way looks too difficult, avoid the temptation to start at the end and work your way backwards. This technique would violate the rules and could result in the thief being set free.

Cover Maze: The winning cake has been stolen: Investigate the evidence and find a clear path to the end of the trail.

Introduction

We live in a day and age when all kinds of crimes are committed. Throughout large cities and in many small towns, crimes occur all too often. Fortunately, men and women enter the profession of law enforcement to help solve crimes and protect the innocent. This is especially necessary in large communities, but in outlying areas and in small rural towns where there aren't enough law enforcement officers, the average person must keep his or her eyes open for any wrongdoing.

To qualify to be a law enforcement officer is difficult and requires a lot of education and specialized training. A high level of honesty and integrity is mandatory. A good knowledge of law is necessary, and the proper use of various types of equipment is needed.

Detectives are members of the law enforcement community who investigate crimes. They obtain information and evidence following the crimes, and help solve them. Would you like to be a detective? It could be dangerous, and will require some training. It will be important to look for clues and gather evidence along the way. Above all, you will have to be certain of your findings in order to arrest the guilty and not the innocent.

On the following pages, you will have the opportunity to try your skills at detective work after a crime has been committed. See how well you do at finding out who committed the crime. Be careful not to guess or jump to any conclusions until all the facts are in.

Good luck. Hopefully, you'll be able to solve the crime.

The Setting

It is time for the annual county fair, and everyone is getting excited. Of all the events, the biggest one is the Great Cake Bake contest. Last year's winner will surely cook up his super-secret best recipe with the hope of taking another first-place blue ribbon. But the competition will be tough, and many great cooks are hoping for an upset. They're busy pulling out old down-home recipes and cooking their cakes carefully. The smell of freshly baked cakes is filling the air throughout the community.

But criminal activity has taken place. Someone is stealing the cakes! Who would ever guess that someone would break in and steal cakes from some of the contestants? Could someone care that much about winning to do something like this? Will this year's county fair be ruined? There is only one thing to do: Find and catch the crook before it's too late. This is where *you* can help.

Gather your detective equipment; then undergo special training and start your investigation. Visit each crime scene. Gather evidence. Set up camera surveillance equipment if necessary. Check out suspects. Finally, use the new surefire method for catching crooks—DNA evidence.

DNA is a code that is specific to each person. No two people can have the same DNA code. Hopefully, you'll be able to gather some of the suspect's DNA. When you compare the suspect's DNA to the evidence you've collected, you'll know who the thief is. Finally, and most difficult, you'll have to catch the thief.

If you succeed and the county fair still has its Great Cake Bake, why don't you prepare your favorite recipe and enter your cake in the fair?

The County Fair

Help set up for the county fair by taking the sign for the Great Cake Bake and placing it at the table in front of the tent. Find a clear path.

Help! Robbery!

Someone has broken into Mary's house and stolen her cake. She's very upset. Take her a tissue by finding a clear path through the garden.

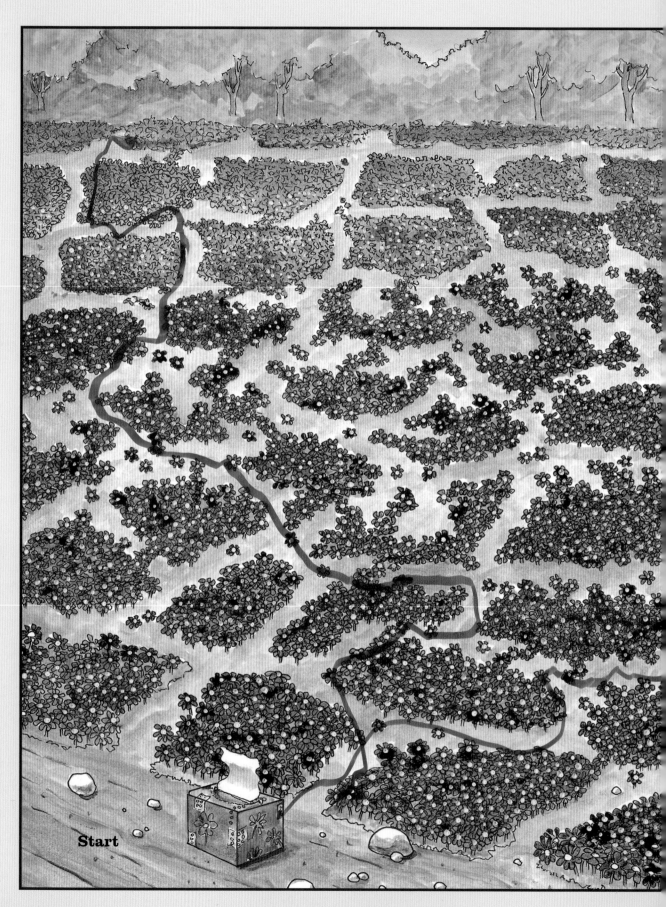

Start

End

Gather Detective Equipment

To become a detective, you'll need detective equipment. Stay on the blue tiles and visit each table once. Get search permits at the clipboard. Don't move on a diagonal or backtrack.

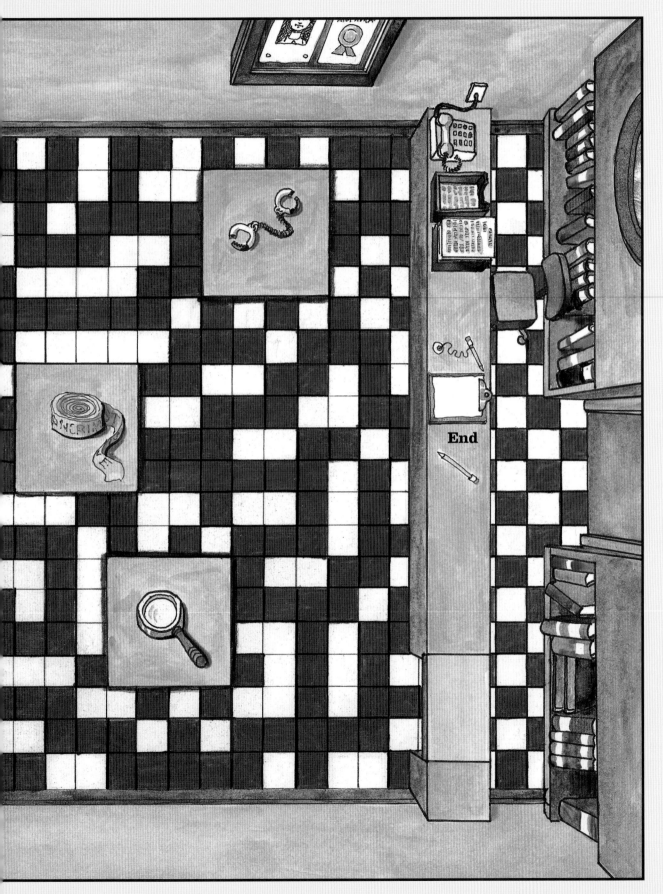

End

Gather Clues

Practice being a detective by learning how to gather clues. Pick up clues by visiting each room once. Don't backtrack or cross over your path.

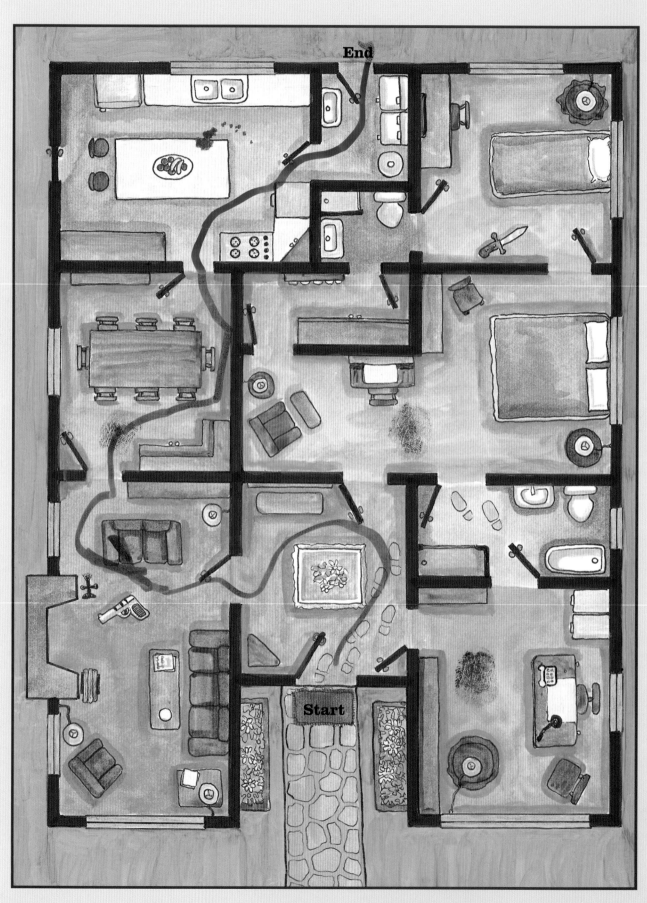

The Lineup

Learn who left the clues from this lineup. Find the path from the clues that leads to the bad guy.

Another Break-In

It's time to go to work because another cake has been taken. Find a clear path to the farmer's house and put the yellow crime tape on the posts around the house.

Start

Camera Surveillance

It's likely that more cakes will be stolen. To get a picture of the thief, place a camera outside each house. Visit each house once. Don't backtrack or cross over your trail.

Start

Crime Scene 3

Another cake is missing. Investigate the crime scene, look for clues, and pick up the film cassette from the black box near the cake dish.

Start

End

Crime Scene 4

Looks like another theft. Keep your eyes open for clues and find your way to the black box.

Start

End

Crime Scene 5

The cake thief has struck again. Find a clear path through the garden area to the break-in and retrieve the film cassette from the black box just inside the broken window.

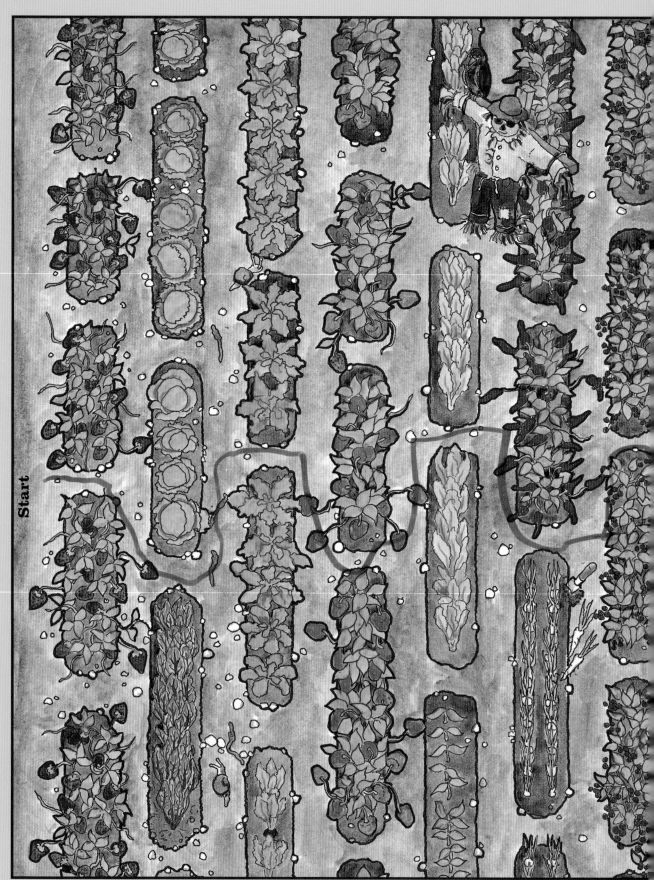

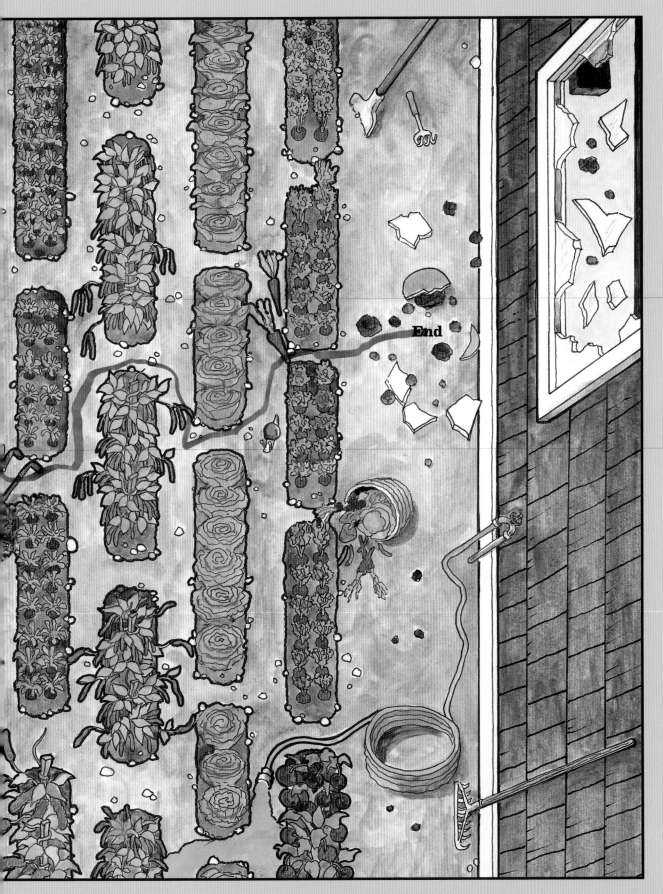

End

Crime Scene 6

There'll be no cake contest unless this thief is caught. There is some blood, which will be good for a DNA test. Find a clear path to the black box and get the pictures.

Start

End

Crime Scene 7

Find a clear path to the black box. After you get this film cassette, gather together *all* of the pictures.

Start

End

The Film Results

Could the thief be the raccoon, the ballplayer, last year's Great Bake winner, the bear, or the snoopy neighbor? Follow every path from each house to the pictures. Place the

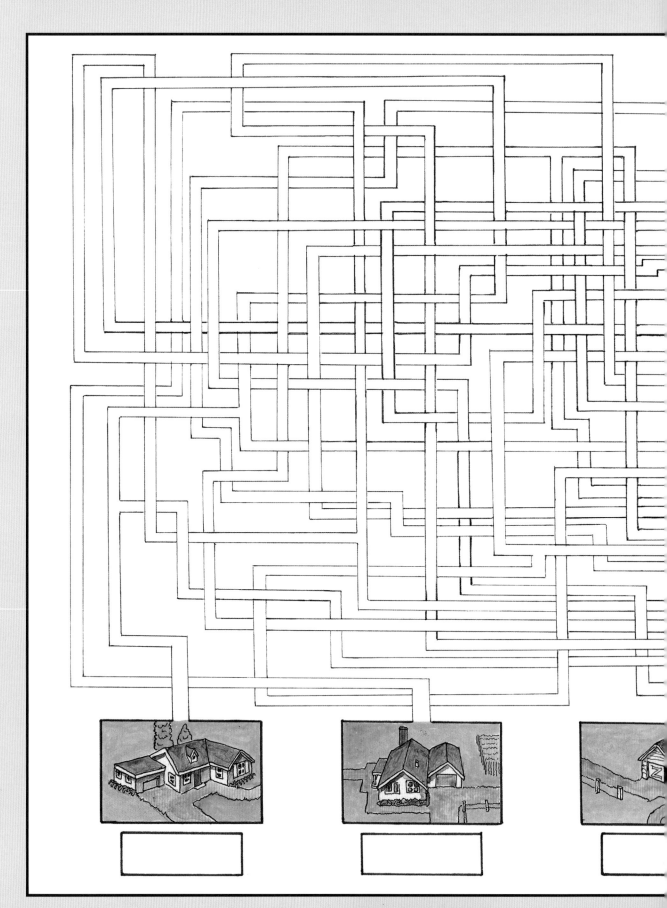

numbers of the suspects in the box below each house. Several suspects could appear at a single house. Then analyze your results.

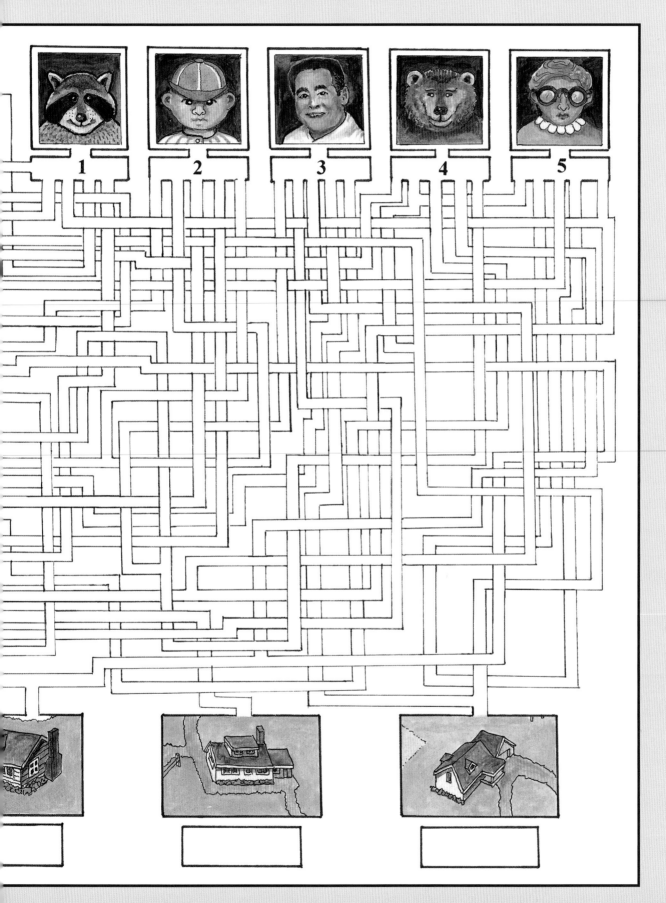

Last Year's Winner

Begin to gather DNA from the suspects. Find a clear path to the house of last year's winner.

Start

End

The Cookbook Library

Find a clear path around the cookbooks to the kitchen.

The Kitchen

You can get DNA from the spoon and the glass. Find a clear path around the flour spilled on the floor. Notice that the cake for last year's winner has not been stolen. Is that a clue?

The Ballplayer

Find a clear path and pick up the soda can on the bench. It will contain the ballplayer's DNA.

Start

End

The Snoopy Neighbor

Find a clear path to her house.

Start

End

The Stairs

Find a clear path up the stairs littered with her children's toys to the bathroom.

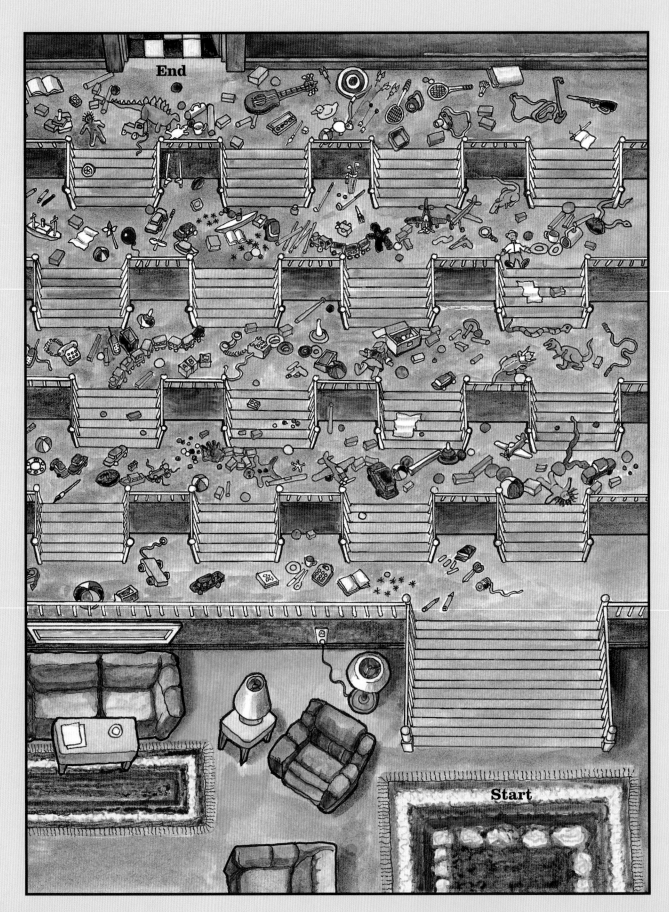

The Bathroom

Stay on the white tiles to pick up the toothbrush. Don't step at a diagonal.

The Raccoon

Hike down through the tree roots and pluck a hair from the raccoon's tail. You have to stay on one root system. Do not cross over onto an overlapping root.

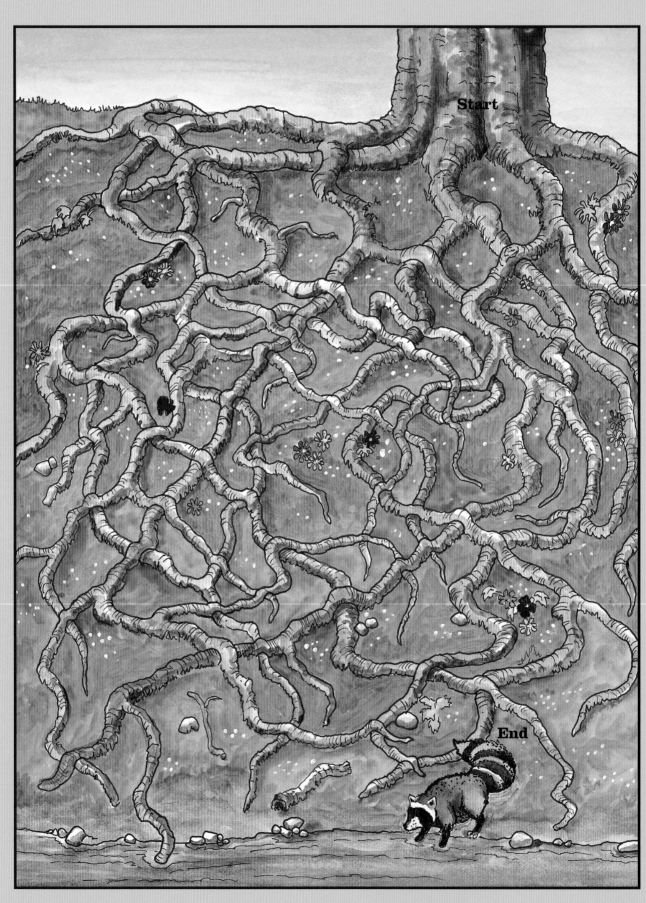

The Bear

The bear has scratched his back on that tree, leaving behind hairs. Find a clear path to the tree.

DNA Results

This is it! The DNA results of the blood left at the crime scene are complete. The suspects' DNA samples also have been collected. Look carefully for the one that matches. Track each result to the suspect. Now you should know who the thief is.

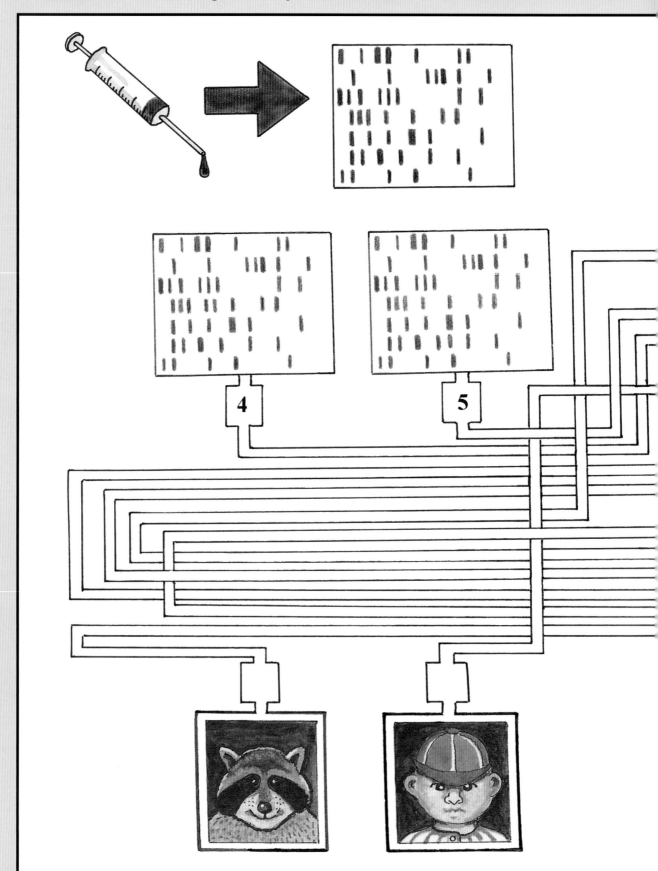

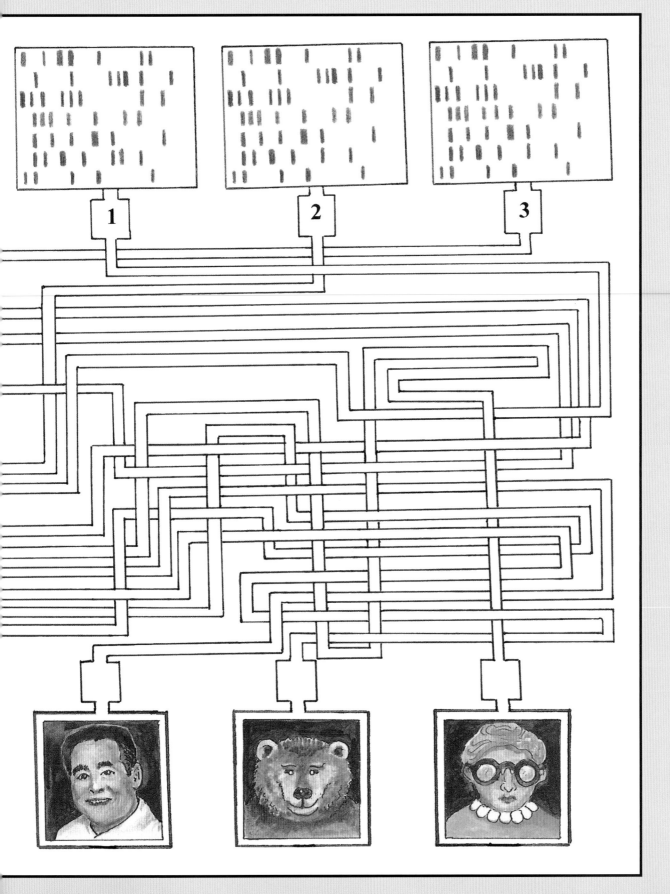

Capture the Thief

That's him in the cave. Take the cage and find a clear path to the cave.

Start

End

Haul Him Away

Take the thief far enough away so that he will never be a problem again. Find a clear road.

Start

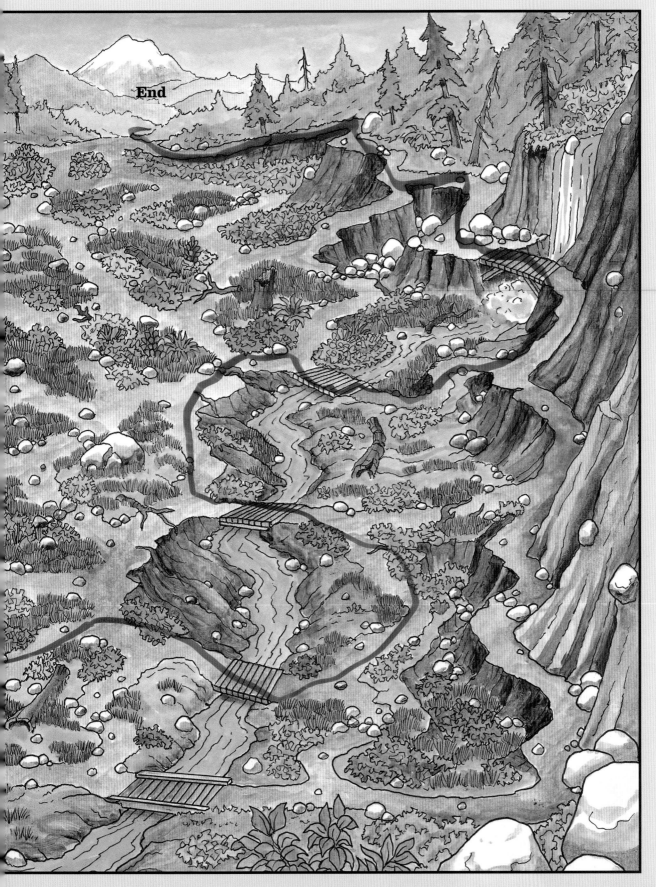

End

Bake Your Cake

Get your blueberry swirl cake ready for the fair. Put the ingredients into the bowl in the correct order. Start at the top and trace the path to the empty box above the bowl so that you will know which ingredient goes in first.

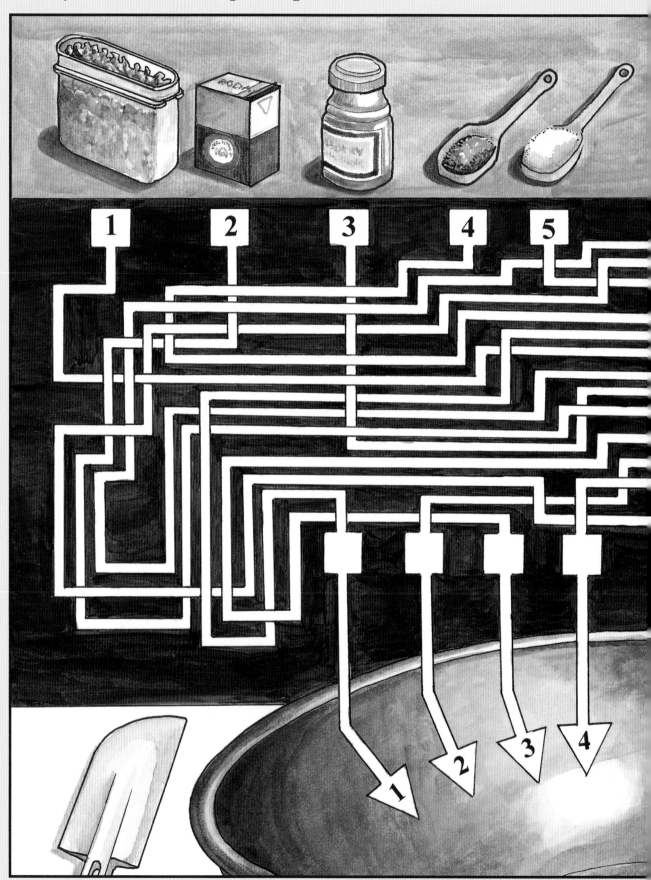

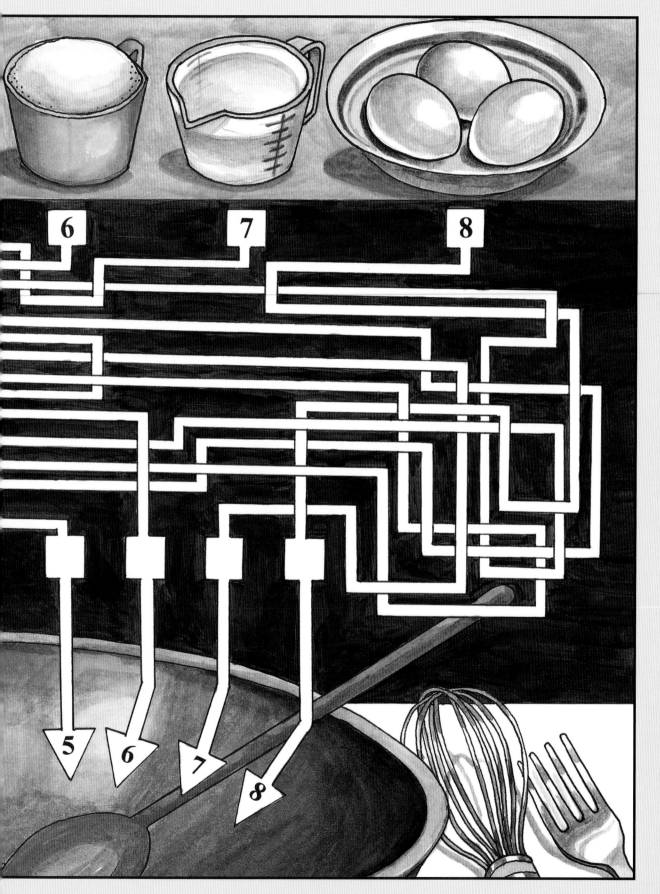

And the Winner Is?

Who won? Was it Paul, last year's winner, the ballplayer, you, the snoopy neighbor, or the farmer? Find out who took first, second, third, and honorable mention by following each ribbon's path to the cakes.

Congratulations!

Congratulations on solving the great mystery of who was breaking in and taking all of those wonderful cakes. You went about your investigation carefully, gathered evidence, and didn't come to any conclusions until all the evidence was in. You made sure you were right before you placed any blame. You concluded that the raccoon was at the crime scene eating leftover crumbs. Last year's winner just wanted to borrow ingredients. The ballplayer wanted his ball back, and the snoopy neighbor wanted to see what was happening. You successfully caught the thief, which was the bear, and dealt out justice fairly by taking him far enough away so that he would not cause any more trouble. Thanks to your good work the county fair was able to have its Great Cake Bake.

Oh, yes, and congratulations on winning the first-place blue ribbon—that's really great! But there's one question remaining . . .who stole your cake?

If you had any problems finding your way, refer to the maze solutions on the following pages.

Cover Maze / The County Fair

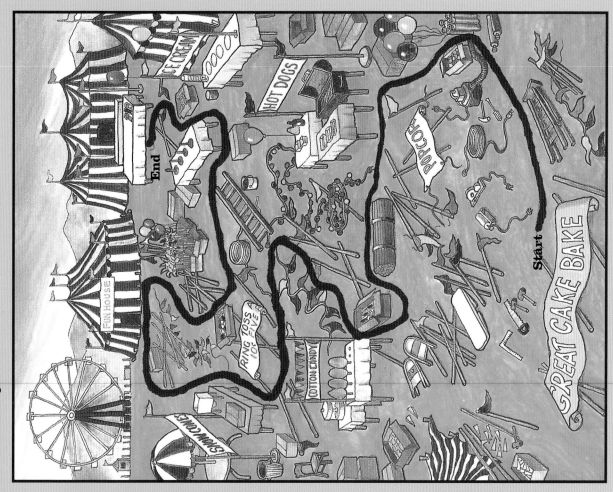

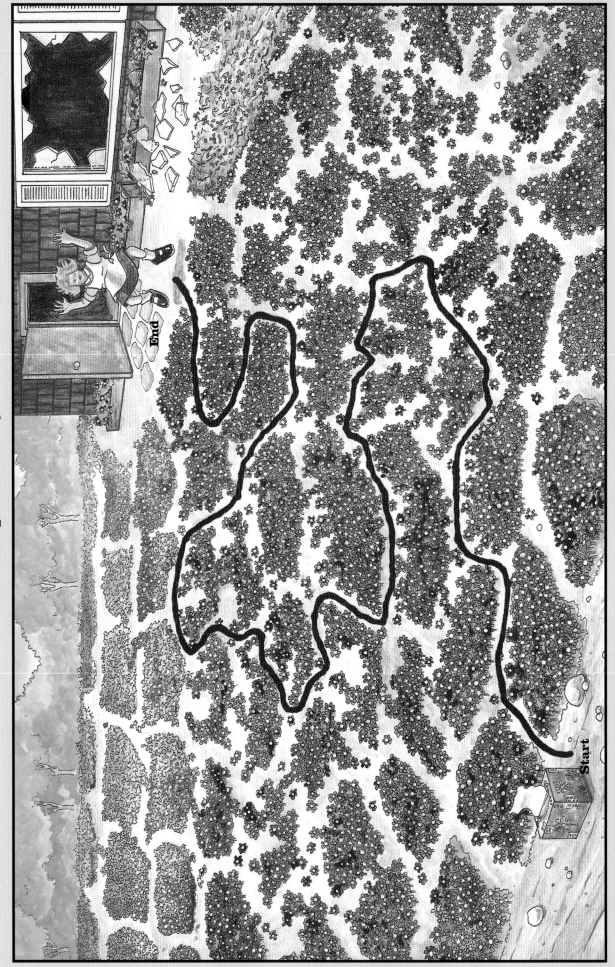

Help! Robbery!

Start

End

Gather Detective Equipment

Gather Clues

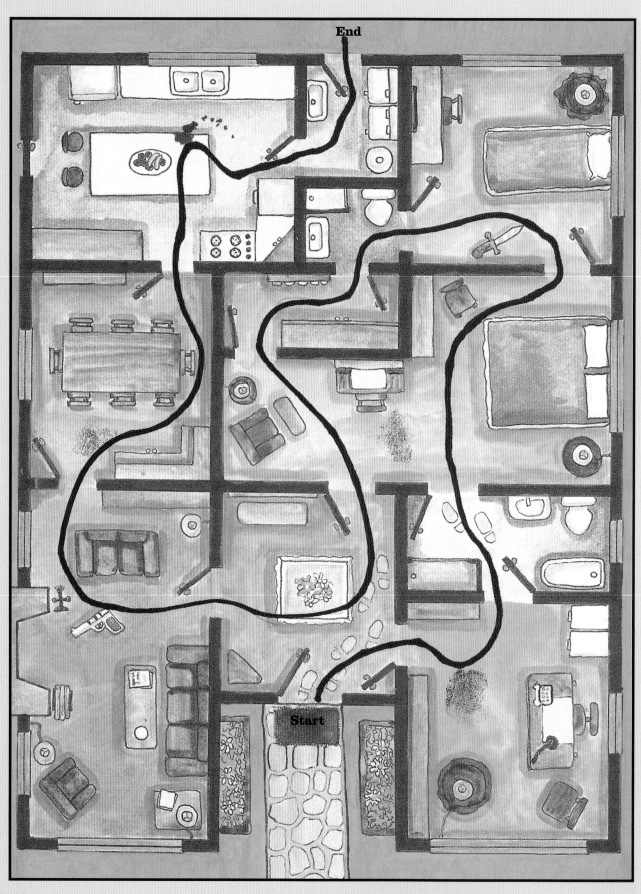

The Lineup

Another Break-In

Start

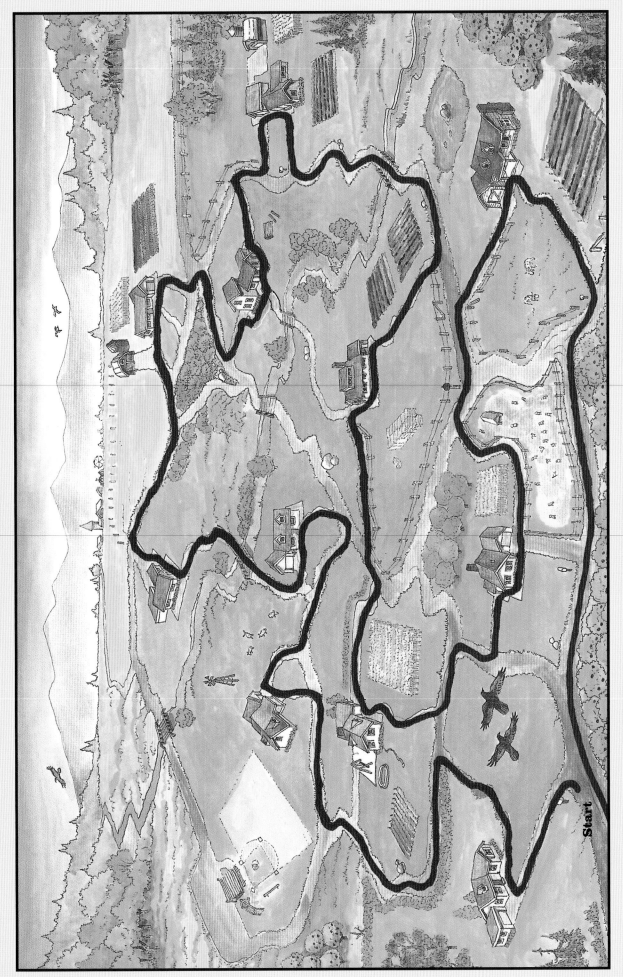

Camera Surveillance

Start

Crime Scene 3

End

Start

Crime Scene 4

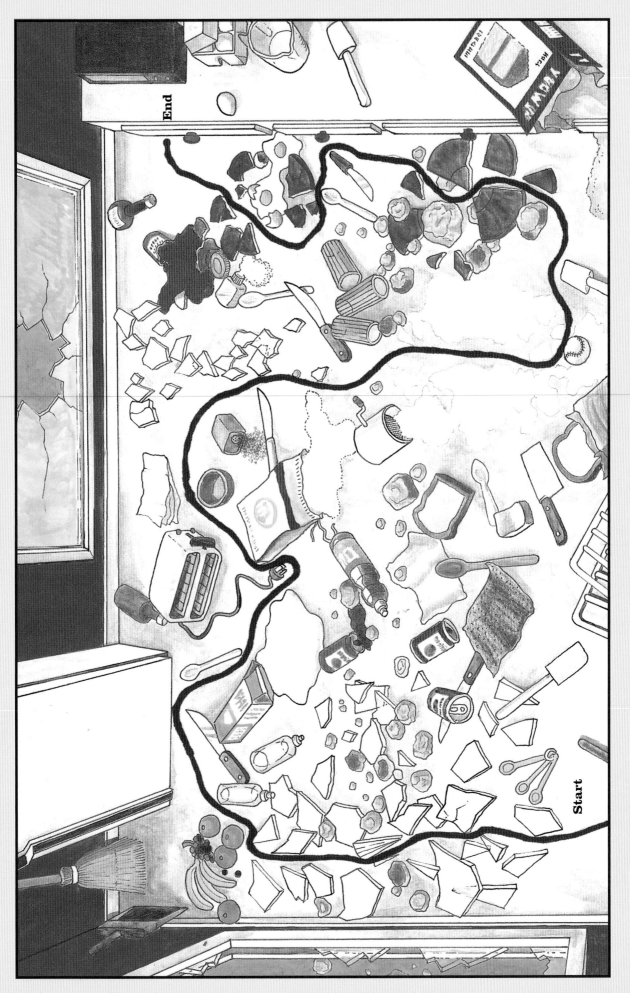

End

Start

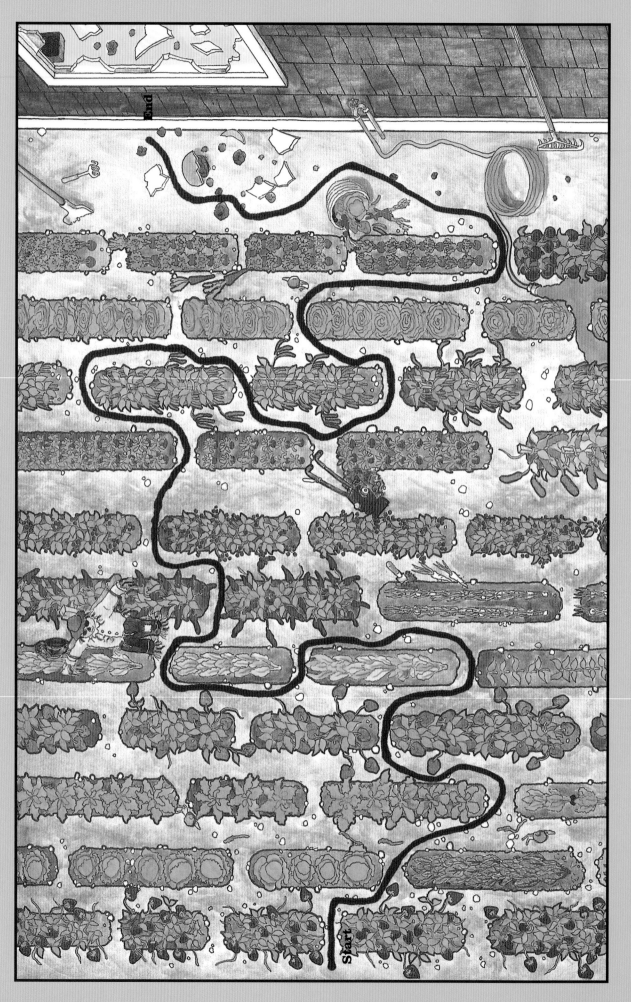

Start

End

Crime Scene 7

Start

End

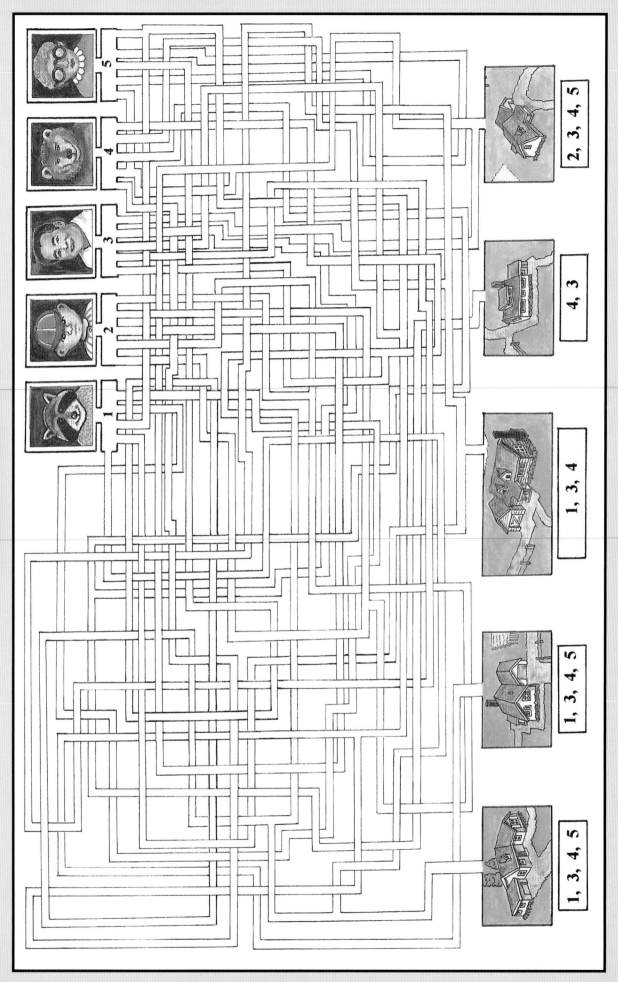

Last Year's Winner

End

Start

The Cookbook Library

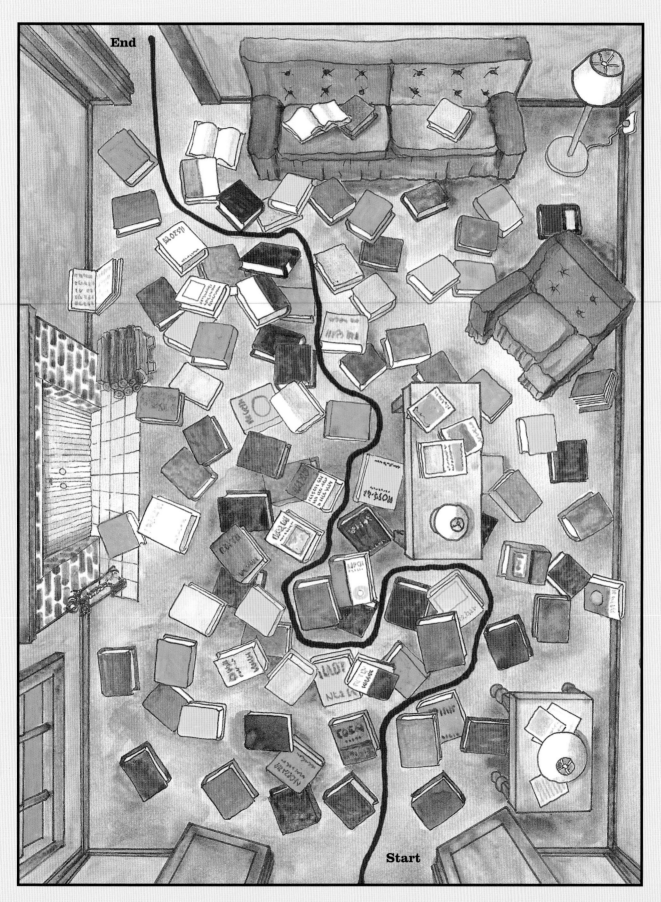

The Kitchen

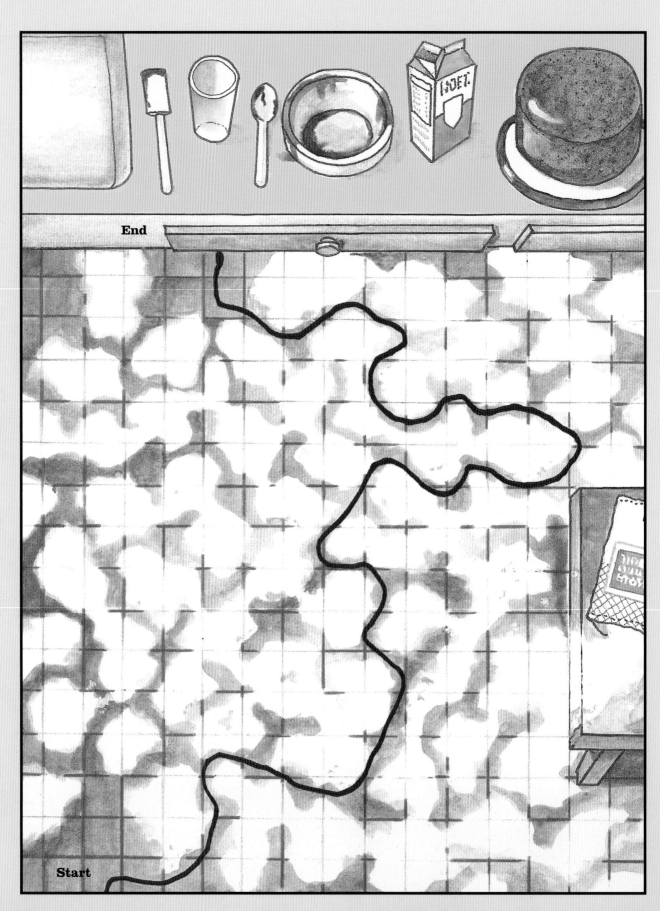

The Ballplayer

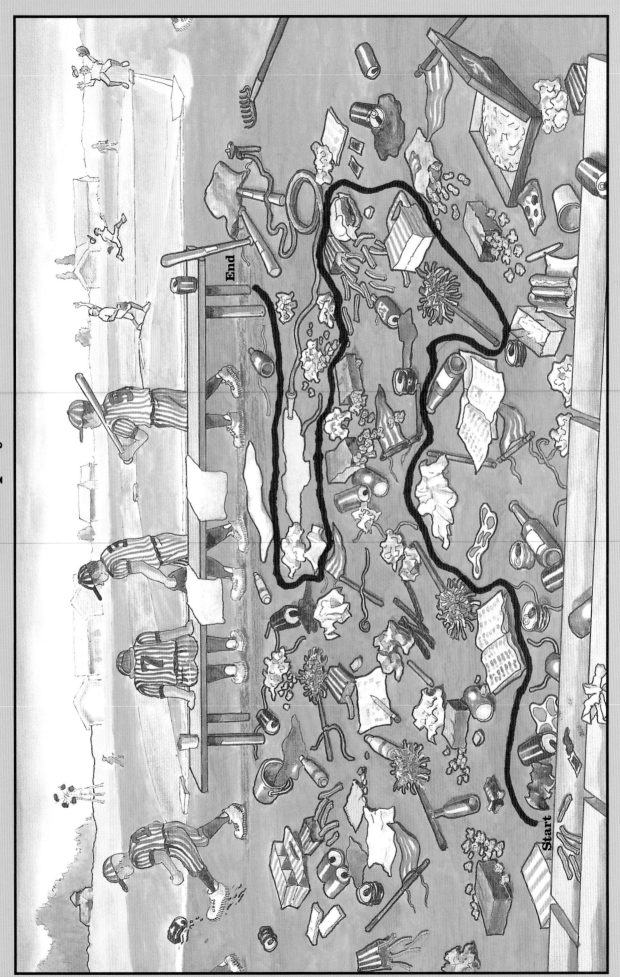

The Snoopy Neighbor

End

Start

The Stairs

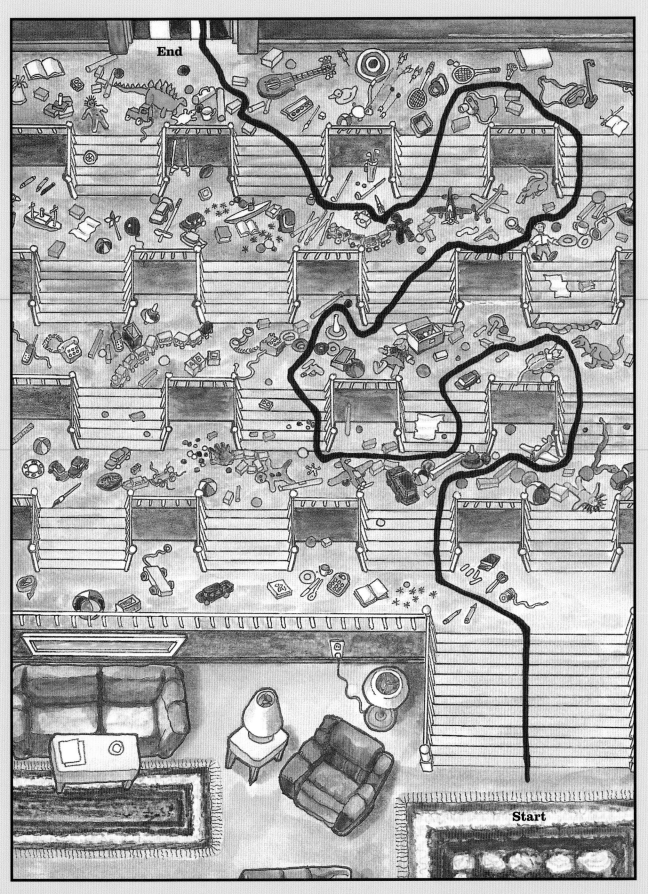

End

Start

The Bathroom

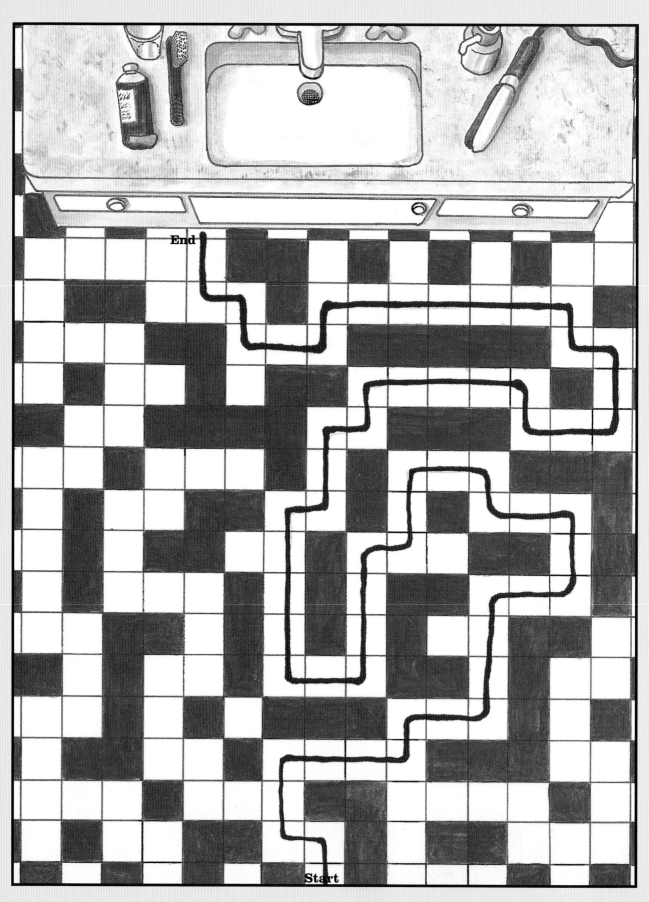

The Raccoon

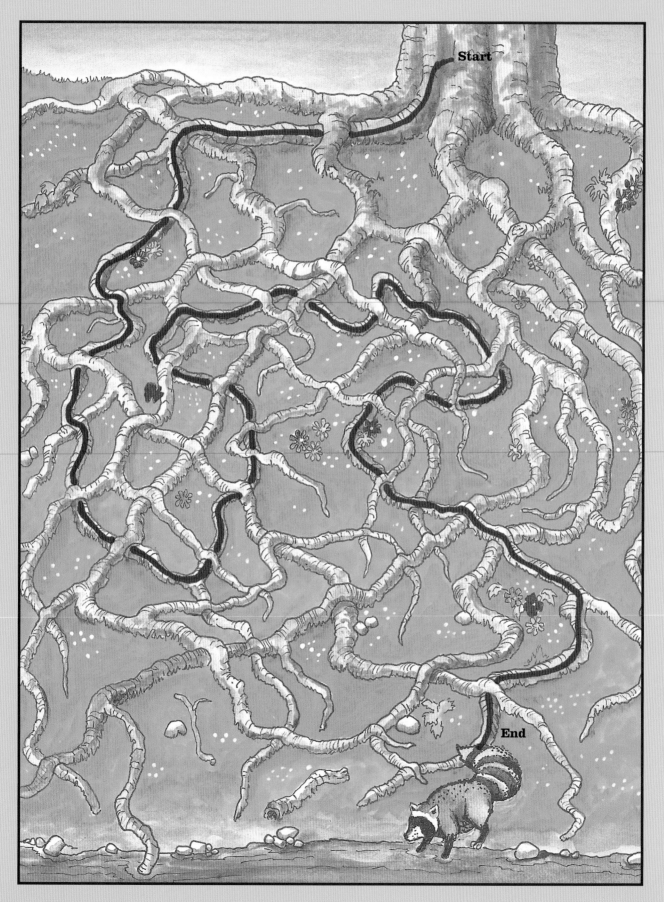

Start

End

The Bear

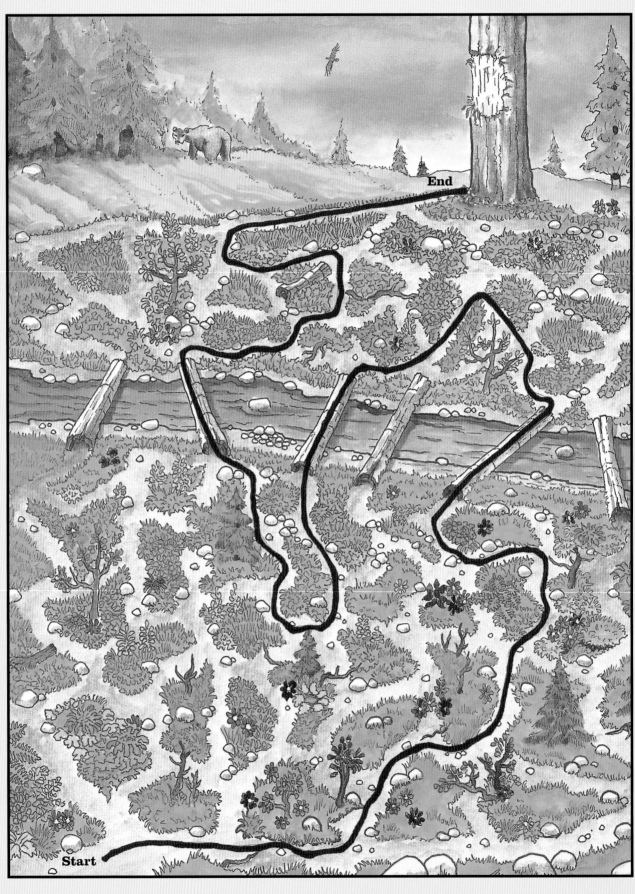

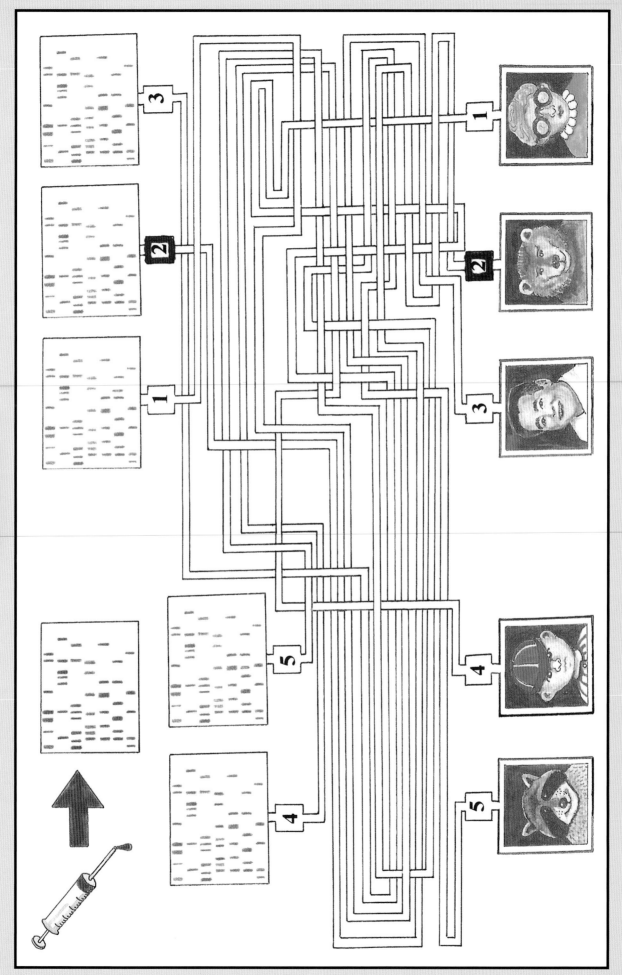

Capture the Thief

Start

End

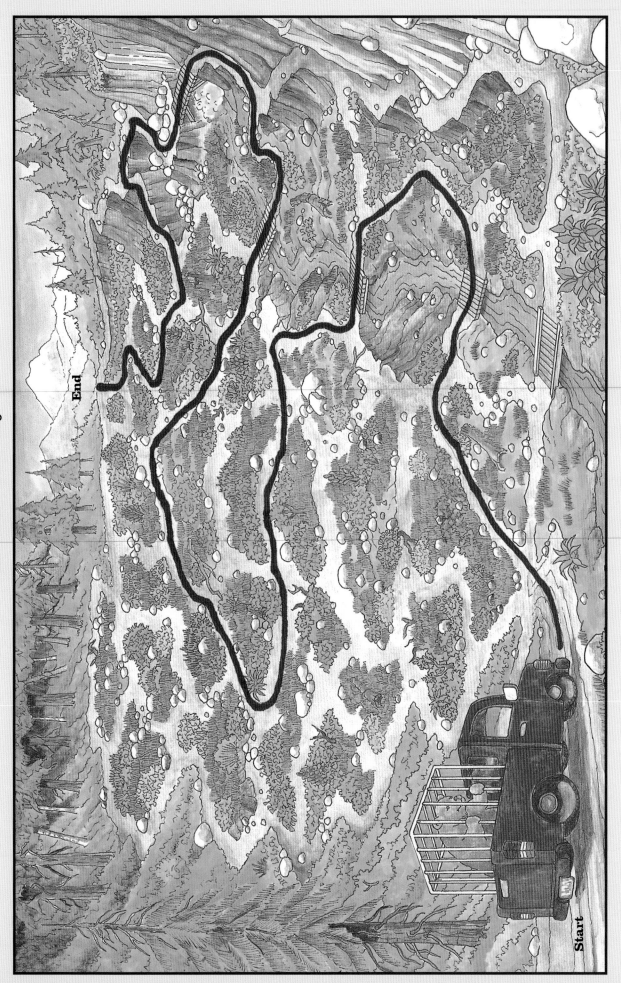

Haul Him Away

End

Start

Bake Your Cake

And the Winner Is?

Index
Pages in **bold** refer to answer mazes

Maze Books by Roger Moreau

Around the World Mystery Mazes:
 An A-maze-ing Colorful Adventure!
Dinosaur Escape Mazes: An A-maze-ing
 Colorful Adventure
Dinosaur Mazes
Great Escape Mazes
History Mystery Mazes: An A-maze-ing
 Colorful Adventure!
Lost Treasure Mazes
Mountain Mazes

Natural Disaster Mazes
Space Mazes
Treasure Hunt Mazes: An A-maze-ing
 Colorful Journey!
Undersea Adventure Mazes: An A-maze-ing
 Colorful Journey!
Volcano & Earthquake Mazes
Wild Weather Mazes
Wizard Magic Mazes: An A-maze-ing
 Colorful Quest!